PRESENTED TO

_____

_____

FROM

D1056807

The

Soul

of the

Quran

INSPIRING
PRAYERS TO KINDLE
HEART AND MIND

Compiled by
SANIYASNAIN KHAN

GOODWORD BOOKS

For Mohammad Rafiq Lodhia

First published 1998
Reprinted 2013
© Goodword Books 2013

Goodword Books
1, Nizamuddin West Market, New Delhi-110 013
Tel. 9111-4182-7083, 4652-1511
email: info@goodwordbooks.com
www.goodwordbooks.com

Islamic Vision Ltd.
434 Coventry Road, Small Heath
Birmingham B10 0UG, U.K.
Tel. 121-773-0137
e-mail: info@ipci-iv.co.uk
www.islamicvision.co.uk

IB Publisher Inc.
81 Bloomingdale Rd, Hicksville
NY 11801, USA
Tel. 516-933-1000
Toll Free: 1-888-560-3222
email: info@ibpublisher.com
www.ibpublisher.com

Printed in India

"When My servants ask you about Me, tell them that I am near. I answer (every) prayer of those beseeching Me when they call upon Me; therefore, let them listen to My call and put their trust in Me, that they may be rightly guided."
(2:186)

INTRODUCTION

Any person who has become conscious of the Existence and Presence of Allah (the meaning of the word 'Muslim') has experienced the most important and heart-shaking of experiences. Suddenly, the world and that individual's place in it takes on a completely different aspect and meaning. In fact, maybe for the first time, that individual realises that the universe and his or her place in it actually has a meaning.

So many people wander through their journey of earthly life without discovering what that meaning is—they are born, grow, eat and drink, mate, age and die, without ever realising that their physical components of atoms are as minute and insignificant as those of one tiny ant lost on a huge planet; but these atoms are only the temporary belongings of a soul which inhabits a vastly different plane of existence.

The realm of *al-Ghayb*, that which is Unseen and Unknown to us within the limitations of our human lives, is vast indeed. A Muslim becomes a Muslim when some inkling of that Reality enters his conscious mind. This awareness may steal in gently as the invisible air we breathe, or it may break through our envelope of ignorance like a flash of lightning. The person may never have thought about Allah at all, or realised that the faith of others was relevant; or that person may have prayed routinely and out of familiar duty for years. The moment of realisation, if it comes, is different for each individual.

But once it comes, life has changed forever for that individual. It is not only the overwhelming realisation that there really is a God, an Almighty and Supreme Being, but that the power and 'heart' of this Being created and maintains all that exists, encompasses the entire vastness of all the universes, and yet at the same time is aware not only of each person as an individual, but of each ant, and of each microbe that may live within the body of that ant.

When Muslims pray using the physical movements of their bodies, they are acknowledging certain things. Firstly, as they stand quietly before Allah, shutting out 'the world,' they are realising their absolute helplessness and insignificance in the light of their Creator's Presence, and they are overwhelmed with the need to ask forgiveness for their shortcomings that took place in those moments when they were not aware. Then, in humility, they bow as they draw closer to consciousness of that Great Being's almightiness and power. Then, as they feel the Divine Love and Compassion flood their souls, they kneel with their faces on the earth, and love Him in response.

Prayer is an acknowledgment of our absolute dependence on Allah on the one hand, as opposed to Allah's absolute power on the other. The act of prayer puts us in our true place, and also acknowledges Allah's rightful station.

Prayer, then, is not the wishful thinking or illusions of the pious but is actually acceptance of things as they are; in prayer-consciousness is the ultimate degree of realism; and the apprehension of, reality, in turn, is the most excellent of all actions. For, in this world, where we have been given a choice between belief and disbelief, there is nothing greater than acceptance of the true nature of things which lies beyond the consciousness of those who are merely living on the animal level.

Although He is the Great Almighty lord of all that is, Allah declares of Himself in the Qur'an that He is *sami ad-dua or* 'One Who hears all prayer' (14:39), and is so close to us that He uses the image of running in our own bloodstream, closer to us than our own jugular vein (50:16). He urges us over and over again to pray to Him, to place our trust in Him, to turn over the motivation of our lives to Him, that we may prosper both in this world and the life to come.

The following selections of prayers and passages about prayer in the Qur'an show how prayer is the lifeline of the true believer.

*P*raise be to Allah,
Lord of the Universe,
the Beneficent, the Merciful,
Master of the Day of Judgement.
You alone we worship,
and to You alone we turn for help.
Guide us to the straight path.
The path of those who have found
Your favour,
not of those who have incurred
your wrath, nor of those
who have gone astray.

(1:1-7)

*T*his Book—let there be no doubt it—
contains sure guidance for those
who have reverence for God;
who believe in the Unseen,
are steadfast in prayer,
and spend (on others)
out of what We have provided for them;
and who believe in the revelation bestowed upon
you (O Prophet)
as well as that sent before your time;
and have firm belief in the life Hereafter.
It is they who follow the guidance from their
Lord,
and it is these who will prosper.

(2:1-5)

O people! Worship your Sustainer
who created you and those who came before you,
so that you may have the chance
to learn righteousness.

(2:21)

$\mathcal{B}$e steadfast in prayer;
practise regular charity; and bow down your
heads with all those who bow down.
Do you ask other people to behave rightly,
while forgetting (to do it) yourself, even though
you recite the holy words?

(2:43-44)

$\mathcal{M}$ake yourselves strong with patience
and prayer.
It is indeed hard, but not to those
who are humble in spirit,
who know that they will meet their lord
and that to Him they will return.

(2:45-46)

*T*ruly, those who have faith (in this
Quran), as well as those who follow the
Jewish (faith),
and the Christians and the Sabians—all
who believe in God and the Last Day,
and do righteous deeds,
shall have their reward with their Sustainer;
they need have no fear,
neither shall they grieve.

(2:62)

Then your hearts became hardened
thereafter and are like rocks, or even harder;
for there are rocks from which rivers come gushing
and others split, so that water issues from them,
and others tumble down in the fear of God.

(2:74)

Be steadfast in prayer
and pay the zakat regularly;
and whatever good deed you send ahead
for your own souls, you shall find it with God;
for God sees well all that you do.

(2:110)

To God belongs the East and the West;
Wherever you turn, there is God's countenance.
God is All-embracing, All-knowing.

(2: 115)

*A*ccept this from us, Lord. You are
the All-hearing, the All-knowing;
and, our Lord, make us submissive to You,
make of our descendants
a nation that will submit to You;
and show us our ways of worship,
and turn towards us with mercy;
surely You are forgiving and merciful.
Lord, send among them a Messenger, of their own,
who shall recite to them Your revelations,
and teach them the Book and the Wisdom,
and purify them of sin;
You are the All-mighty,
the All-wise.[1]

(2:128-129)

---

[1] PRAYER OF THE PROPHET ABRAHAM (IBRAHIM ﷺ AND ISHMAEL (ISMAIL ﷺ)
WHILE BUILDING THE KA'BAH.

When My servants question you
about Me, tell them that I am near.
I answer the prayer
of every suppliant who calls to Me;
therefore let them respond to Me,
and believe in Me,
that they may be
rightly guided.

(2:186)

*R*emember Me, and I will
remember you;
and be thankful to Me;
and never deny Me.
Believers,
seek help in patience and prayer.
God is with those who
patiently persevere.

(2:152-153)

*S*urely We will try you
with something of fear and famine,
with loss of property and life and crops;
yet give good news
to those who endure with patience;
who say, even when smitten by adversity,
'Surely we belong to God,
and to Him we shall return;'
On such people
will be God's blessing and mercy;
such people are those
who are rightly guided.

(2:155-157)

Your God is One God.
There is no deity save Him,
the All-merciful,
the All-compassionate.

(2:163)

There are those who pray,
Our Lord, give us (what we desire)
in this world,'
but they shall have no share
in the world to come.
And there are others who pray,
'Our Lord, give us what is good
both in this world and in the world to come,
and guard us against the torment of the Fire.'
These shall have a share,
according to their deeds.
God is swift
in His reckoning.

(2:200-201)

God is watching over His servants, those who say, 'Our Lord, we believe in You; forgive us our sins, and save us from the torment of the Fire'—and who are patient, steadfast,
self-controlled, truthful, devout, and charitable,
and who pray for God's forgiveness at daybreak.

(3:15-17)

Celebrate the praises of God
during the appointed days (after the Hajj).
But the one who hastens to leave within two
days shall incur no blame,
and the one who stays longer
shall incur no blame, provided his aim is
to do right.
Then remain conscious of God,
and know that you will surely
be gathered unto Him.

(2:203)

God will not call you
to account
for oaths which you may have uttered
without thought,
but will take you to task
for the intention
in your hearts.
And He is
Oft-forgiving, Most Merciful.

(2:225)

Guard strictly your (habit) of prayers,
especially the Middle Prayer; and stand
before God in a devout (frame of mind).
If you are in danger, pray on foot,
or riding (or in whatever state is convenient at
the time);
but when you are once more secure,
celebrate God's praises
in the manner He has taught you,
which you did not know before.

(2:238-9)

Lord, fill our hearts
with steadfastness.
Make us firm of foot
and help us against the people
who deny the truth.

(2:250)

*A*llah: there is no deity save Him,
the Living, the Everlasting.
Slumber seizes Him not, neither sleep;
to Him belongs all that is in the heavens
and the earth.
Who is there that shall intercede with Him
save by His leave?
He knows what lies before and behind all people.
They can comprehend only that part
of His knowledge which He wills.
His Throne extends over the heavens and earth;
the preserving of them does not weary Him.
He is the All-high, the All-glorious.

(2:255)

To God belongs all
that is in the heavens and the earth.
Whether you bring into the open
what is in your hearts or conceal it,
God will call you to account for it.
He will forgive whom He will,
and chastise whom He will;
God has power over all things.

(2:284)

Whether you conceal what is in your hearts
or bring it out into the open,
Allah knows it all;
He knows what is in the heavens
and what is on earth,
and He has power
over everything.

(3:29)

God does not charge a soul with more
than it can bear.
It shall be requited for whatever good
and whatever evil it has done.
Our Lord,
take us not to task
if we forget, or lapse into error.
Our Lord,
charge us not with the burden
You laid upon those before us.
Our Lord,
do not burden us
beyond what we have the strength to bear.
And pardon us,
and forgive us our sins,
and have mercy on us;
You alone are our Protector.
And help us against people
who deny the truth.

(2:286)

Our Lord, do not cause our hearts to go
astray after You have guided us.
Grant us Your own mercy;
You are the generous Giver.
Lord, You will surely gather all humanity
before You upon a day that will indubitably come.
God will not break His promise.

(3:8-9)

$\mathcal{L}$ord, Sovereign of all sovereignty,
You bestow power on whom You will
and take it away from whom You please;
You exalt whoever You will
and abase whoever You please.
In Your hand lies all that is good;
You have power over all things.
You cause the night to pass into the day
and the day into the night;
You bring forth the living from the dead
and the dead from the living.
You give without measure to whom You will.

(3:26-27)

$\mathcal{O}$ur lord! We believe in what You
have revealed, and we follow the Messenger;
so write us down among those
who bear witness.[1]

(3:53)

---

[1] PRAYER OF THE DISCIPLES OF THE PROPHET JESUS (ISA ﷺ)

Say: O people of the Book! Seek out
the common ground between us and you:
that we shall worship none but God,
and that we shall not ascribe divinity to
anything besides Him;
and that we shall not
take human beings for our lords beside God.'
If they turn (from this), then say:
'Bear witness that (it is) we who have
surrendered unto God's will.

(3:64)

Our Lord! Forgive us our sins
and the lack of moderation in our doings.
Make our steps firm,
and help us against those
who deny the faith.

(3:147)

*I*f God helps you,
none can overcome you;
if He should forsake you,
who is there, after that,
who could help you?
In God, then, let believers
put their trust.

(3:160)

*V*ie with one another, to earn the
forgiveness
of your Lord, and a Paradise
as vast as the heavens and the earth,
prepared for the God-fearing,
who give alms both in prosperity and adversity
and restrain their anger, and forgive
their fellows (God loves the charitable);
who, if they commit an indecency
or wrong their souls,
earnestly fill their minds with God,
and ask forgiveness for their sins—
and who shall forgive sins but God?—
and do not knowingly persist
in their misdeeds.
Their recompense is forgiveness from their Lord,
and gardens beneath which rivers flow,
where they shall dwell forever;
blessed is the reward for those who do
good works.

(3:133-136)

Do not lose heart or fall into despair;
you are bound to gain mastery,
if you are true in faith.

(3:139)

It was part of the mercy of God
that you dealt gently with them (O Prophet);
for if you had been harsh or hard of heart,
they would have broken away from you.
So pass over their faults, and pray
that God may forgive them; and consult them
in all matters of public concern.
Then, when you have taken a decision,
place your trust in God, for God loves
those who put their trust in Him.

(3:159)

God is never unjust
by as much as the weight of an atom;
if there is any good deed (done)
He will multiply it,
and give out of
His grace a great reward.

(4:40)

*S*urely, in the creation of the heavens and
earth, and in the alternation of night and day
there are signs for people of sense,
(those) who remember God, standing and sitting
and lying down to sleep, and reflect upon
the creation of the heavens and the earth:
Our Lord, You have not created this (universe)
in vain. Glory be to You!
Save us from the suffering of the Fire.
Our Lord, those whom You will cast
into the Fire, You will put to eternal shame;
and the evildoers shall have no helpers.
Our Lord, we have heard the call of one calling
us to the true faith, saying,
"Believe in the Lord!" And we believed.
Our Lord, forgive us our sins
and remove from us our bad deeds, and
take our souls to Yourself with the righteous.
Our Lord, grant us what
You have promised us

through Your Messengers, and save us from
disgrace on the Day of Resurrection;
You will never break Your promise!'
And their Lord answers them: 'I will deny no
man or woman among you the reward of their
labours. You are the offspring of one another...'

(3:190-195)

*W*hy should you not fight in the cause
of God and of utterly helpless men,
women and children, who are crying (in prayer):
'O our Sustainer! Rescue us from this town,
whose people are oppressors;
and raise for us, out of Your grace,
someone who will protect us,
one who will bring us help!'

(4:75)

$\mathcal{S}$ay: 'My prayer, my worship,
my living, my dying are for God alone,
the Lord of all Being.'

(6:162)

O believers! Do not attempt to pray
while in a state of drunkenness; wait
until, you can understand all that you are saying;
nor in a state requiring total ablution until you
have washed–
except if you are merely passing by.
But if you are ill, or are travelling,
or have come from answering a call of nature,
or have been sexually intimate,
and can find no water–then take resort to clean
sand, and pass it lightly over your faces and
hands.
God blots out your sins and forgives,
again and again.

(4:43)

O believers! When you prepare for
prayer, wash your faces, and your hands and arms
to the elbows; and pass your hands lightly
over your heads, and (wash) your feet

up to the ankles. If you are in a state requiring
total ablution,
bathe your whole body. But if you are ill,
or are travelling,
or coming from answering a call of nature,
or have had sexual contact, and can find no water,
then take resort to clean sand or dust,
and pass it lightly over your faces and hands.
Allah does not wish to impose any difficulty
on you, but only wishes to make you pure,
and to bestow on you the full measure
of His blessings, so that you
may have cause for gratitude.
And remember the blessings God has
bestowed on you, and His solemn pledge
by which He bound you to Himself,
when you said: 'We hear and we obey.'
So, reverence Allah, for He knows well
the secrets of your hearts.

(5:7-8)

$\mathcal{O}$ believers! Remember the blessings of
Allah toward you when certain people
were about to lay hands on you,
but (God) held back their hands from you.
So reverence Allah, and in Allah let believers
put their trust.

(5:12)

God will say: 'O Jesus, the son of Mary!
Did you ask people to worship you
or your mother as deities beside God?'
He will say: 'Glory to you! Never could I say
what I had no right to say.
Had I said such a thing,
You would indeed have known it.
You know (all) that is in my heart,
though I do not know what is in Yours.
You know in full everything that is hidden.
I never said to them anything except
as You commanded me to say,
"Worship God, my Sustainer and your Sustainer;"
and I bore witness to what they did
so long as I dwelt among them.

But since You took me up, You alone
have been their Keeper,
and You are the Witness to all things.
If You punish them, they are Your servants.
If you forgive them, You are the Exalted in
Power,
the Wise.'[1]

(5:119-121)

Praise be to Allah, Who created the heavens
and the earth, and made the darkness and
the light. Those who reject faith,
hold (other entities) as equal
with their Guardian-Lord.
He it is Who created you from clay,
and then decreed a stated time-span (for you)–
a term known only to Him.
And yet you have doubt within yourselves!
He is God in the heavens and on earth.
He knows all that you keep secret
as well as all that you do openly,
and He knows that which you deserve.

(6:1-3)

With Him are the keys to the things
beyond a created being's perception, the treasures
that none knows but He.
He knows all that is on land and in the sea.
Not a leaf falls, but He knows it;
there is not a grain in the darkness of the
earth, nor anything fresh or withered but it is
recorded
in (His) clear decree.
It is He who takes your souls by night, and
has knowledge of all that you did during the day;
by day He raises you up again, that the time-span
appointed to you may be fulfilled.
In the end, you will return to Him;
then He will show you the truth
of all that you did.
He is the Irresistible,
(watching) from above over His servants;
and He sends forth heavenly forces to watch over
you,

until, when death approaches any of you,
Our angels will take his soul,
and they never overlook (anyone);
Then are people returned to God, their Protector,
the Reality.
Is not His the Command?
And He is the Most Swift in taking account.
Say: 'Who is it that delivers you
from the dark recesses of land and sea,
when you call upon Him humbly,
and in the secrecy of your hearts:
'If only He will deliver us from these (distresses),
we shall most certainly show our gratitude."
Say: 'It is Allah Who can deliver you
from these and all distresses; and yet (some of) you
still ascribe divinity to other powers besides Him.

(6:59-64)

$\mathcal{T}$hose who reject Our messages are deaf
and dumb, in the midst of profound darkness;
God leaves to wander whom He wills,
and He places whom He wills on the Way
that is Straight.
Say: 'Can you imagine yourselves
calling on any
but Allah when His chastisement
comes upon you,
or the last Hour? Give a truthful reply!
No—on Him alone would you call;
and if it be His will, He may remove (the
distress)
which occasioned your call upon Him;
and you will forget all that which you now
think of
as divine besides Him.'

(6:40-41)

*S*ay: 'Shall I seek for my Sustainer other than Allah, when He is the Cherisher of all things?

Every soul draws the reward of its acts on none but itself; no bearer of burdens can bear the burden of another.

In time, to your Sustainer you must return; and then He will make you truly understand all the things you used to argue over.'

(6:164)

*L*ord, we have wronged our souls. Pardon us and have mercy on us, or we shall surely be among the lost.

(7:23)

Say: 'My Lord has commanded justice,
and that you turn to Him
whenever you kneel in prayer
and call on Him, with true devotion.
As He created you in the beginning,
so shall you return.'

(7:29)

Pray to your Lord, humbly and in private;
He does not love transgressors.
Do not spread corruption on the earth,
after it has been so well ordered.
Pray to Him with awe, and with hope.
His mercy is (always) within the reach
of the righteous.

(7:55-56)

Lord, give us patience and
let us die in submission.

(7:126)

$\mathcal{L}$ord, You alone are
our Guardian.
Forgive us and have mercy on us:
You are the noblest of
those who forgive.
Ordain for us what is good,
both in this life and
in the Hereafter.
To You alone we turn.

(7:155-156)

And prescribe for us what is good
in this world, and in the world to come;
we have repented to You.'
He replied, 'My chastisement—I smite with it
whom I will; and My mercy embraces all
things, and I will show mercy to those who
are God-fearing,
spend in charity and who believe in Our
message.

(7:156)

To God belong the Names Most Beautiful;
so call Him by them, and keep away
from those who blaspheme His Names–
they shall assuredly be punished for their
misdeeds.

(7:180)

It was He who created you out of one
living soul and out of it brought into being its
mate,
so that he might find comfort in her. Then,
when he had lain with her, she conceived,
and for a time her burden was light.
She carried it with ease
but when it became heavy
they prayed to Allah their Lord,
If You give us a righteous son,
we shall be truly thankful.'
Yet when He had given them a righteous son,
they set up other deities besides Him,
in return for what He had given them;
Exalted is Allah above what they associate (with
Him).

(7:189-190)

The true believers are those
whose hearts tremble with awe
whenever God is mentioned;
when His revelations are recited to them,
it increases them in faith,
and in their Lord they put their trust;
those who are constant in prayer ,
and spend on others
out of what We have provided them.
Those are the true believers.
They will be exalted and forgiven by their
Lord,
and a generous provision
shall be made for them.

(8:2-4)

*R*emember your Lord deep
in your soul, with humility and reverence
and without ostentation,
in the morning and in the evening;
and do not be negligent.
Surely those (angels) who are near your Lord
are never too proud
to worship Him;
they extol His praise,
and to Him they bow.

(7:205-206)

*R*emember you were praying
to your Sustainer for help,
and He answered you:
'Truly, I will send to your aid a thousand
angels, rank upon rank.'
God made this a message of hope,
that your hearts may be set at rest;
there is no help except from Allah,
the Exalted in Power, the Wise.

(8:9-10)

*K*now that God is
your Protector–an excellent Protector,
an excellent Helper!

(8:40)

*I*f you do not help him[1],
God will help him as He helped him
when the unbelievers drove him–
he being the second of two
When the two were in the cave, he said
to his companion[2], 'Do not despair.
God is with us.'
Then God sent down His mercy, and
sent to his aid unseen forces and
He made the word of the unbelievers the
lowest;
and God's word the uppermost;
God is All-mighty, All-wise.

(9:40)

---

1. THE PROPHET MUHAMMAD ﷺ.
   2. ABU BAKR.

*T*hose who repent,
those who serve and praise Him,
those who fast,
those who journey
in devotion to the cause of Allah,
those who bow,
those who prostrate themselves in prayer,
those who encourage justice
and forbid evil,
those who keep God's commandments.
So give these good tidings to the believers.

(9:112)

It is He who enables you to traverse
land and sea. They embark: and as the ships
set sail with a fair breeze, they rejoice in it;
then, when there comes upon them a strong
wind, and waves come on them from every
side, they fear they are being overwhelmed by
death.
They call upon God, sincerely offering (their)
duty to Him saying,
'If You deliver us from this peril
we shall be truly thankful.'
But when He has delivered them, see–
they behave outrageously on earth.
O people, your insolent deeds
corrupt your own souls.
You take your enjoyment in this present life:
in the end, to Us you shall return,
and We shall show you the truth of
all that you have done.

(10:22-23)

Lord, do not let us suffer
at me hands of me wicked.
Deliver us, through Your mercy:
from me unbelievers.

(10:85-86)

And perform the prayers
morning and evening,
and at night-time too; surely the good deeds
will wipe out the evil deeds.
That is an admonition for thoughtful people.
And be patient; God will not deny the
righteous their reward.

(11:114-115)

God alone has knowledge of
what the heavens and the earth conceal;
to Him all things shall be referred.
Serve Him, and put your trust in Him.
'Your Lord is never heedless
of the things you do.

(11:123)

God invites you to the Home of Peace,
and He guides whomsoever He will
to a straight path.

(10:25)

$\mathcal{L}$ord, I would prefer to go to prison
than give in to their advances.
Shield me from their cunning,
or I shall yield to them and lapse into folly.1
So his Lord answered his prayer,
and He turned away from him their guile;
He is the All-hearing,
the All-knowing.

(12:33-34)

$\mathcal{H}$e said, 'I complain to God
of my sorrow
and my sadness.
God has made things known to me
that you know not.'2

(12:86)

---

1 THE PRAYER OF THE PROPHET JOSEPH (YUSUF ﷺ) WHEN HE WAS
   CONFRONTED WITH WOMEN OF THE EGYPTIAN NOBILITY AND WAS
   THREATENED WITH BEING SENT TO PRISON.

2 THE PRAYER OF THE PROPHET JACOB (YAQUB ﷺ) WHEN HIS BELOVED SON,
   BENJAMIN WAS HELD IN EGYPT ON THE CHARGE OF THEFT.

$\mathcal{A}$nd he* lifted his father and mother
upon the throne; and the others fell down
prostrate before him. 'See, father,' he said,
'this is the interpretation of my vision
of long ago; my Lord has made it true.
He was good to me when He released me
from the prison, and again
when He brought you out of the desert
after Satan had stirred up strife
between me and my brothers.
My Lord is gentle to whom He will;
He is the All-knowing, the All-wise.
O my Lord, You have given me authority,
and You have taught me to interpret dreams.
Creator of the heavens and the earth,
You are my Protector
in this world and in the next.
Let me die as one who has surrendered himself
to You, and join me
with the righteous.[1]

(12:100-101)

---

* THE PROPHET JOSEPH (YUSUF 达).

God leaves in error whom He will,
and guides those who repent and have faith,
whose hearts find comfort
in the remembrance of God.
Surely in the remembrance of God
all hearts are comforted.
Blessed are those who have faith
and do good works;
blissful is their end.

(13:27-29)

*I*t is God who created the heavens
and the earth,
and sent down out of heaven water.
He brings forth fruits for your sustenance.
He drives the ships which
at His command sail the ocean
in your service.
He has created rivers for your benefit
and has subjected to you the sun and moon
which remain constant upon their courses,
and He has subdued for you the night and day.
He has given you all you asked Him for.
If you reckoned up God's blessings,
you could never count them.
Truly, man is sinful, and ungrateful!

(14:32-34)

We know that you are distressed
by what they say.
Give glory to your Lord and prostrate yourself.
Worship your Lord,
till the certainty comes to you.

(15:97-99)

Do they not see how every object God created
casts its shadow to the right and to the left,
bowing before God in all lowliness?
To God bows everything in the heavens,
and every creature crawling on the earth,
and the angels too.
They are not disdainful;
They fear their Lord on high,
and do what they are commanded.

(16:48-50)

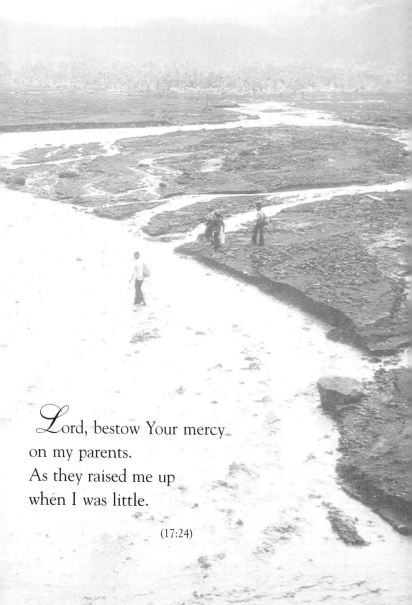

$\mathcal{L}$ord, bestow Your mercy
on my parents.
As they raised me up
when I was little.

(17:24)

Abraham prayed, 'My Lord,
make this land secure, and preserve me
and my descendants from worshipping idols.
Lord, they have led many people astray.
He that follows me shall become my brother,
but if anyone rebels against me, surely You
are All-forgiving, All-compassionate.
Our Lord, I have settled some of my offspring
in a barren valley (Mecca) near Your Sacred
House, so that they may observe true worship.
Put in the hearts of people kindness towards
them, and provide them with the earth's fruits
so that they may be thankful.
Our Lord, You know what we keep secret
and what we reveal;
from God nothing whatever is hidden
in earth and heaven.
Praise be to God, who gave me Ishmael
and Isaac in my old age!

All prayers are heard by Him.
My Lord, make me and my descendants
steadfast in prayers.
Our Lord, accept my prayer.
Our Lord, forgive me and my parents,
and all the believers,
on the Day of Reckoning.

(14:35-41)

*O*ur Lord! Send upon us Your mercy,
and show us the solution to our problem
in the right way.[1]

(18:10)

---

[1] PRAYER OF THE YOUTHS IN THE CAVE.

$\mathcal{L}$ord, grant me a goodly entrance
and a goodly exit,
and sustain me with Your power.

(17:80)

*K*eep your soul content
(along) with those who call on their Lord
morning and evening, seeking His
countenance;
and let not your eyes pass beyond them,
seeking the allurements of this life;
nor pay any heed to those
whose hearts We have rendered heedless
of the remembrance of Us,
who follow their own desires,
abandoning all that is good and true.

(18:28)

An account of your Lord's goodness
to His servant Zachariah:
He called upon his Lord secretly
saying, 'O my Lord, behold
the bones within me are feeble
and my head glows silver with age.
Yet never, O my Lord, has my prayer to You
remained unanswered.
And now I am afraid of my kinsfolk
after I am gone;
and my wife is barren.
Grant me a son
who shall be my inheritor
and an heir to the House of Jacob,
and who will find grace in Your Sight.'
'Rejoice Zachariah, We give you
good tidings of (the birth) of a son,
whose name shall be Yahya (John).
Never have We given this name to anyone
before him.

(19:2-7)

These are the people
to whom God has been gracious:
the Prophets from among the descendants of
Adam, and of those whom We carried with Noah;
the descendants of Abraham and Israel,
and of those whom We have guided and chosen.
When the signs of the All-merciful
were recited to them,
they fell down prostrate, in tears.

(19:58)

*W*e did not reveal the Qur'an to you
from on high to make you unhappy,
but only to encourage the God-fearing.
It is a revelation from Him
who created the earth and the lofty heavens,
the Merciful who sits enthroned on high.
To Him belongs all that is in the heavens
and the earth and all that is between them,
and all that is underneath the soil.
You have no need to speak aloud,
for He has knowledge (even) of all that is
secret, and all that is hidden.
God–
there is no deity save Him.
His (alone) are the Most Gracious Names.

(20:1-5)

*T*o bear with patience whatever they say,
and give glory to your Lord
before the sunrise, and before sunset.
Praise your Lord in the watches of the night,
and at the ends of the day;
so that you may find comfort.[1]

(20:130)

*T*o Him belongs whosoever is in the heavens
and the earth; and those who stand in His
presence are not too proud to do Him service,
nor do they grow weary,
glorifying Him by night and in the daytime
unflaggingly.

(21:19-20)

---

[1] OUT OF THE FIVE CANONICAL PRAYERS, FOUR ARE DERIVED FROM THIS VERSE, WHILE THE FIFTH ONE IS MENTIONED IN 2:238.

$\mathcal{L}$ord, increase my knowledge.

(20:114)

And Dhu'n-Nun (Jonah)—
when he went away enraged,
thinking that We had no power over him;
then he called out in the darkness,
'There is no deity save You.
Glory be to You!
I have done wrong.'
So We answered his prayer,
and delivered him from distress;
even so do We deliver
the true believers.

(21:87-88)

Say: 'Lord, judge with fairness!'
Our Lord is the Merciful;
His help we seek
against your blasphemies.

(21:112)

And Zachariah–when he invoked
his Lord: 'O my Lord, let me not
remain childless;
though of all heirs You are the best.'
We answered his prayer and gave him John,
curing his wife of sterility.
They vied with one another in good works,
and called upon Us with piety,
fear and submission.

(21:89-90)

And tell of Job (Ayyub):
how he called on his Lord,
saying: 'I am surely afflicted,
but of all those who show mercy,
You are the most merciful.'
We heard his prayer,
and relieved his affliction.
We restored to him his family and many more
with them: a blessing from Ourself
and an admonition to those
who worship.

(21:83-84)

$\mathcal{L}$ord, 'put courage into my heart,'
prayed Moses, 'and ease my task for me.
Free the knot of my tongue,
that they may full understand my message.
Appoint for me among my kinsmen one who
will help me bear my burden,
Aaron, my brother; by him add to
my strength, and let him share with me
in my tasks, so that we may give glory to You,
and remember You without ceasing.
Surely You are watching over us. ,
He replied: 'Your request is granted, O Moses.'

(20:25-36)

O people, bow down and prostrate
yourselves, and serve your Lord,
and do good; so that you may prosper;
and struggle for the cause of God as is His due,
for He has chosen you, and has laid on you
no burden in the observance of your religion,
that being the creed of your father Abraham;
He named you Muslims
in this as in former scriptures
so that the Messenger may be a witness to the
truth before you, and that you may be
witnesses to it
before all mankind. So be constant in prayer,
and pay the alms, and hold fast to God;
He is your Protector–
a gracious Guardian and a gracious Helper.

(22:77-78)

*T*hen, when you go aboard the Ark
with all your followers, say, 'Praise belongs to
God, who has delivered us from a sinful nation.
And say, 'O my Lord, let my landing be
blessed. You alone can make me land in safety.'[1]

(23:28-29)

*L*ord, I seek refuge in You
from the promptings of all evil impulses.
Lord, I seek refuge with You
from their presence.

(23:98-99)

---

[1] THE PRAYER OF THE PROPHET NOAH (NUH ﷺ).

$\mathcal{Y}$our God is One God,
so surrender to Him.
And give good news to the humble
whose hearts are filled with awe
whenever God is mentioned,
who endure patiently
whatever adversity befalls them,
and who perform their prayers,
and give charity of what We have
provided them.

(22:34-35)

Among My servants there were those
who said, Our Lord, we believe;
therefore forgive us,
and have mercy on us,
for You are the best of the merciful.'

(23:109)

Put your trust in the Living God,
who never dies. Extol His limitless glory,
and celebrate His praise.
He is well aware of His servants' sins.
He created the heavens and the earth,
and what is between them, in six aeons,
and is established on His Throne.
He is the Lord of Mercy: ask about Him
the one who is (truly) aware!

(25:58-59)

The true believers are those who pray:
'Lord, give us joy in our spouses and children
and make us foremost among those
who are conscious of You.'
These shall be rewarded for their patient
endurance
with the loftiest abode in Paradise.
There they shall find welcome and greeting,
and there they shall abide for ever: a blessed
dwelling
and blessed resting-place.

(25:74-76)

And say: 'My Lord, forgive
and have mercy , for You are the best
of the merciful.'

(23:118)

Do you not see how God is praised by
those in heaven and those on earth,
even by the birds as they spread out their wings?
Each knows indeed how to pray to Him
and give Him glory; He notes the prayers
and praises of all His creatures,
and has knowledge of all their actions.

(24:41)

God is the Light of the heavens and the earth;
His Light may be compared to a niche
wherein is a lamp (the lamp in a glass,
the glass as it were a glittering star)
kindled from a Blessed Tree,
an olive that is neither of the East nor of the West,
oil of which would give light (of itself),
even if no fire touched it;
Light upon Light;
God guides to His Light whom He will.
And God speaks in metaphors to people.
God has knowledge of everything.
His light is found in the houses of worship
God has allowed to be raised up,
for His Name to be commemorated therein;
therein glorifying Him in the mornings
and the evenings
are people whom neither commerce nor trade
diverts from the remembrance of God
or the performance of the prayer,
or the payment of the alms, fearing
a day when hearts and eyes will be convulsed;

who hope that God may reward them
in accordance with their noblest deeds
and give them out of His grace,
more (than they deserve).
God gives without measure to whom He will.

(24:35-38)

*P*ut your trust in the Almighty,
the Compassionate
who observes you when you stand (alone),
and your behaviour among the worshippers.
Surely He hears all and knows all.

(26:217-220)

*S*urely worthier is He who answers
the oppressed, when they cry out to Him,
and relieves their suffering.

(27:62)

*R*ecount to them the story of Abraham
when he asked his father and his people,
'What is it that you worship?'
They replied, 'We worship idols, and pray to
them with all fervour.'
He asked, 'Do they hear you when you call,
can they help you or do you harm?'
They replied, 'This was what our fathers did
before us.'
He said, 'And have you considered what
you have been worshipping,
you and your forefathers, the elders?
They are my enemies. Not so the Lord of all
the worlds, Who has created me, Who guides me,
and gives me food and drink,
and whenever I am sick, heals me,
Who will cause me to die, and bring me back
to life Hereafter, and Who I hope will forgive
my sins on the Day of Judgement.
My Lord, give me wisdom, and join me
with the righteous,
and grant me the power to convey the truth to
those who will come after me.

Make me one of the inheritors
of the Garden of Bliss, and forgive my father,
for he is one of those astray.
Do not put me to shame
on the Day of Resurrection;
the Day when neither wealth nor offspring
will avail anything
and when none shall be saved except the one
who comes before the Lord with a pure heart.

(26:69-89)

Say: 'Praise be to God,
and peace be on His servants
whom He has chosen.'
Who is more worthy, God
or the idols they serve
besides Him?

(27:59)

Lord, I stand in dire need of any good which You may bestow upon me!

(28:24)

When they came to the Valley of Ants,
an ant said, 'Ants, enter your dwelling places,
lest Solomon and his warriors
should unwittingly crush you!'
But he smiled, laughing at its words,
and said, 'Inspire me, Lord,
that I may forever be grateful for the blessings
You have bestowed on me and on my parents,
and that I may do good works
that will please You;
and include me through Your mercy
amongst Your righteous servants.'

(27:18-19)

And say: 'Praise be to God! He will
show you His signs and you will recognise
them. Your Lord is never unmindful of
anything you do.'

(27:93)

$\mathcal{H}$e prayed, 'My Lord, Forgive me!
for I have sinned against my soul.'
So God forgave him, for He is the All-forgiving,
the All-compassionate.
He said, 'By all the blessings You have shown
me, Lord, I vow that I will never lend a
helping hand to a wrongdoer.'[1]

(28:17-18)

$\mathcal{A}$nd He is God;
there is no deity save Him.
His is the praise
in this world and in the Hereafter.
His is the power supreme,
and to Him you shall be recalled.

(28:70)

---

[1] THE PRAYER OF THE PROPHET MOSES (MUSA ﷺ) AFTER HE ACCIDENTALLY KILLED A FELLOW EGYPTIAN.

Convey what has been revealed
to you of the Book, and be steadfast in prayer;
prayer restrains from indecency and dishonour.
But your foremost duty is to remember God.
God has knowledge of all your actions.

(29:45)

*H*e said, 'My Lord, help me against these people who spread corruption.'[1]

(29:30)

*S*o give glory to God morning and evening.
Praise be to Him
in the heavens and on the earth,
at twilight and at noon.
He brings forth the living out of that which is
dead, and the dead out of that which is alive.
And He gives life again to the earth
after it has been lifeless.
Likewise you shall be raised to life.

(30:17-19)

---

[1] THE PRAYER OF THE PROPHET LOT (LUT ﷺ).

*N*one believe in Our revelations save
those who, when reminded of them,
fall down prostrate
and proclaim the praise of their Lord,
in all humility;
who forsake their beds to pray to their Lord
in fear and hope; who give in charity of that
We have provided them.

(32:15-16)

*M*en and women who have surrendered,
believing men and believing women,
obedient men and obedient women,
truthful men and truthful women,
enduring men and enduring women,
humble men and humble women,
men and women who give in charity,
men who fast and women who fast,
men and women who guard their chastity ,
men and women who are ever mindful of God—
on them God will bestow forgiveness
and a rich reward.

(33:35)

$\mathcal{B}$elievers, be ever mindful of God;
praise Him at the dawn and in the evening.
It is He and His angels who bless you,
to bring you forth from the darkness into the light.
He is Compassionate to the true believers.
Their greeting, on the day when they meet Him,
will be 'Peace!' And He has prepared for them
a generous reward.

(33:41-43)

$\mathcal{O}$ people, remember God's blessing upon you;
is there any creator, apart from God, who
provides for you out of heaven and earth?
There is no deity save Him.
How then can you turn away?

(35:3)

God has now revealed
the best of scriptures,
a Book uniform in style
proclaiming promises and warnings.
Those who fear their Lord tremble with awe
at its revelations,
and their skins and hearts melt
at the remembrance of God.

(39:23)

Say: 'Lord, Creator
of the heavens and the earth,
knower of the Unseen and the Visible,
You alone can judge
the disputes of Your servants.'

(39:4-6)

*H*a Mim.
This Book is revealed by God
the Almighty, the All-knowing,
Forgiver of sins, Accepter of repentance.
Severe in retribution,
limitless in His bounty,
there is no deity save Him,
and to Him is the final return.

(40:1-3)

*S*ay: 'Servant of God, you that have sinned against your souls, do not despair of God's mercy; for He forgives all sins. He is the Forgiving, the Compassionate.

Turn in repentance to your Lord and surrender to Him, before the suffering overtakes you; for then there will be none to help you.

Follow the best of what has been revealed to you by your Lord, before the punishment comes upon you suddenly while you are unaware.'

Lest any soul should say, "Alas for me, I have disobeyed God, and scoffed at His revelations."

Or: "If only God had guided me, I should have been among the God, fearing."

Or, when he sees the suffering (that awaits him): "O that I might return again, and be among the righteous."

For God will say to him, "Yes indeed! My signs did come to you, but you denied them. You were arrogant and had no faith at all."'

(39:53-59)

Those who fear their Lord shall be
led in bands to Paradise.
When they draw near,
its gates will be opened,
and its keepers will say to them:
'Peace be to you; you have led good lives.
Enter Paradise and dwell in it for ever.'
They will exclaim: 'Praise be to God
who has fulfilled His promise to us and has
I bestowed upon us this vast region as an
inheritance so that we may make our abode in the
Garden wherever we please.
How excellent is the reward of the righteous.
And you shall see the angels
circling round the Throne,
giving glory to their Lord.
They shall be judged with fairness,
and all shall say,
'Praise be to God, Lord of the Universe.'

(39:73-75)

So be patient;
God's promise is true.
And ask forgiveness for your sins, and
proclaim the praise of your Lord
in the evening and at dawn.

(40:55)

Lord, Your mercy and knowledge
embrace all things.
Forgive those who repent and follow Your path.
Shield them from the suffering of Hell.
Admit them, Lord, to the gardens of bliss
which you have promised them,
together with all the righteous among their fathers,
their wives, and their descendants.
You are the Almighty, the Wise One.
Deliver them from all evil.
He whom You will deliver from evil on that day
will surely earn Your mercy.
That is the supreme triumph.

(40:7-9)

Your Lord has said, 'Call on Me
and I will answer you.'

(40:60)

The heavens well-nigh break apart above
them,
as the angels give glory to their Lord,
and ask forgiveness for those on earth.
God–is the Forgiving, the Merciful.

(42:5)

It is He who accepts repentance
from His servants, and pardons evil deeds;
He has knowledge of all your actions.
And He answers those who believe
and do righteous deeds, and enriches them
through His bounty .
And the unbelievers–for them awaits
a terrible punishment.

(42:25-26)

It is He who has made the earth
a resting-place for you, and traced out routes
upon it that you may find your way;
who sends down water from the sky in due
measure;
and thereby resurrects dead land;
(even thus you shall be raised to life)
and who has created all living things in pairs,
and made for you ships and beasts on which you
ride,
so that, as you mount upon their backs,
you may recall your Lord's blessing,
and say, 'Glory be to Him,
who has subjected these to us.
We ourselves were not
able to subdue them.
To our Lord we shall all return.'[1]

(43:10-14)

---

[1] PRAYER: GLORY BE TO HIM...' IS OFTEN RECITED WHILE MOUNTING AN
ANIMAL, DRIVING A CAR OR BOARDING A SHIP OR AEROPLANE.

It is He who sends down rain for them
when they have lost all hope,
and He unfolds His mercy;
He is the Protector, worthy of all Praise.

(42:28)

We indeed created man;
and We know the promptings of his soul,
and We are nearer to him
than his jugular vein.

(50:16)

Hear then whatever they say,
and proclaim your Lord's praise
before the rising of the sun, and before its
setting, and Praise Him in the night,
and make the additional prostrations.
(50:39-40)

I have not created jinn and mankind
except to worship Me.
I demand no livelihood of them,
neither do I ask that they should feed Me.
God alone is the All-provider,
the Possessor of Strength, the Invincible.

(51:56-58)

*B*e patient and wait for the judgement
of Your Lord;
We are watching over you.
And proclaim the praise of your Lord
when you awaken,
and proclaim the praise of your Lord
in the night, and at the declining of the stars.

(52:48-49)

We have charged man, that he be kind
to his parents; his mother bore him painfully,
and painfully she gave birth to him.
He is born and weaned in thirty months.
When he is fully grown,
and reaches forty years,
let him pray, 'Inspire me, my Lord
mat I may be thankful for Your blessing
bestowed on me and my parents,
and mat I may do good works mat will please
You; Grant me good descendants.
To You I turn and to You
I surrender myself.'

(46:15)

So prostrate yourselves before God,
and worship Him!

(53:62)

Help me, Lord, I am overcome!

(54:10)

This is the indubitable truth.
Then magnify the Name of your Lord,
the Almighty.

(56:95-96)

We created you; will you not believe?
Have you considered the seed you spill?
Did you yourselves create it, or are We
the Creators? We have decreed death among you;

nothing can hinder Us from replacing you
by others like yourselves or transforming you
into beings you know nothing of.
You have known the First Creation; so why
do you not reflect! Consider the seeds you grow.
Is it you that give them growth, or We?
If We pleased, We could turn your harvest
into chaff, so that filled with wonderment, you
would exclaim: 'We are laden with debts;
surely we have been robbed!' Have you
considered the water you drink?
Did you send it down from the clouds,
or did We send it!
If We pleased, We could make it bitter;
so why are you not thankful?
Have you considered the fire you kindle?
Did you make its timber grow, or did We?
We Ourselves made it as a reminder,
and a boon to the desert-dwellers.
Then magnify the Name of your Lord, the
Almighty.

(56:57-74)

The All-merciful has taught the Qur'an,
He created humanity
and taught articulate speech.
The sun and the moon pursue their ordered
course,
and the plants and the trees bow down in
adoration.
The heavens–
He raised on high and set the balance.
Transgress not in the balance,
give just weight and full measure.
And the earth–He laid it down for
His creatures, with all its fruits,
and blossom-bearing palm-trees,
and grain in the blade,
and fragrant herbs.
O which of your Lord's blessings
would you deny?

(55:1-13)

Strive for the forgiveness of your Lord,
and for a Paradise as vast as heaven and earth,
prepared for those who believe
in God and His Messengers.
Such is the bounty of God;
He gives it to whomsoever He will;
and God's bounty is infinite.

(57:21)

O believers, fear God, and put your trust
in His Messenger. He will give you
a twofold portion of His mercy,
and bestow on you a light to walk in,
and He will forgive you;
God is All-forgiving, All—compassionate.

(57:28)

Allah has indeed heard the prayer
of the woman who plead's with you
concerning her husband,
and carries her complaint to Allah.
And Allah always hears the arguments
between both sides among you;
for He hears and sees everything.

(58:1)

Forgive us Lord,
and forgive our brothers who
embraced the Faith before us.
Do not put in our hearts
any malice towards the faithful.
Lord, You are compassionate
and Merciful.

(59:10)

$\mathcal{O}$ believers, when the call is made
for Friday prayers hasten to God's remembrance
and cease your trading.
That is better for you, if you but knew it.
Then, when me prayers are finished, disperse
and go on your way in the quest of God's
bounty, and remember God always;
so mat you may prosper.

(62:9-10)

Lord, in You we have put our trust;
to You we turn and to You we shall come at last.
Lord, do not expose us
to the designs of the unbelievers.
Forgive us, Lord, You are the Mighty, the
Wise One.

(60:4-5)

Believers, turn to God in true repentance;
it may be that your Lord will forgive you your
sins, and admit you into gardens underneath which
rivers flow, on a day when the Prophet
and those who believe with him will suffer no
disgrace at the hands of God.
Their light will shine in front of them,
and on their right; and they will say,
'Our Lord, perfect our light for us,
and forgive us.
You have power over all things.'

(66:8)

*B*lessed be He who in His hands
holds all sovereignty.
He has power over all things.
He created death and life,
that He might put you on trial
and that which of you is fairest in works;
He is the Almighty, the Forgiving–
who created seven heavens, one above the
other.
You will not find a flaw in the creation of the
Merciful.
Turn up your eyes: can you detect a single flaw?
Then look again, and yet again,
your eyes in the end will grow dim and weary .

(67:1-4)

*W*hether you speak secretly or aloud,
He knows your inmost thoughts.
Shall He not know, who created?
And He is the Subtle, the All-knowing.

(67:13-14)

$\mathcal{L}$ord, build me a house
with You in Paradise.

(66:11)

We have sent down to you the Qur'an
by gradual revelation;
so await with patience the judgment of your
Lord,
and do not yield to the wicked and the
unbelieving.
Remember the Name of your Lord at dawn
and in the evening and part of the night;
bow down before Him and magnify Him
through the long night.

(76:23-26)

Again, you shall surely see it (Hell)
with the eye of certainty.
Then you shall be questioned on that day
about the blessings.

(102:7-8)

But those who believe, and do righteous
deeds, are the best of creatures;
their recompense is with their Lord–
the Gardens of Eden, underneath which rivers
flow, therein dwelling for ever.
God is well-pleased with them,
and they are well-pleased with Him;
Thus shall the God-fearing be rewarded.

(98:7-8)

Surely We have given you abundance;
so pray to your Lord and sacrifice to Him.
It is surely your opponent who will be ruined.

(108:1-3)

Say: 'He is Allah, One,
Allah, the Eternal,
who has not begotten,
nor has He been begotten.
There is none comparable to Him.

(112:1-4)

$\mathcal{O}$ soul at peace, return to your Lord,
well-pleased, well-pleasing!
Join My servants!
Enter My Paradise!'

(89:29-30)

When the help of God and victory come,
and you see people entering God's religion
in their thousands,
then proclaim the praise of your Lord,
and seek His forgiveness;
for He is ever disposed to mercy.

(110:1-3)

Say: I take refuge in the Lord of the daybreak:
from the evil of what He has created,
from the evil of darkness when it gathers,
from the evil of conjuring witches,
from the evil of an envier when he envies.'

(113:1-5)

Say: 'I take refuge in the Lord of men.
The King of men, the God of men,
from the evil of the slinking prompter
who whispers in the hearts of men;
from jinn and men.'

(114:1-6)